What is a Mind?

John King

123 Books

Copyright © 2011 by John King

All rights reserved. This book, or parts thereof, may not be reproduced in any form without permission.

A catalogue record for this book is available from the British Library

ISBN: 978-1-907962-29-5

Published by 123 Books

Reading, England

For Dolph

Contents

Preface		7
Introduction		9
1	A central core of human attributes?	15
2	Freedom?	23
3	Feeling States?	28
4	Perception?	37
5	Intentionality?	49
6	Awareness?	58
7	The Inner Cause of Certain Movements in Suitable Circumstances?	69
8	Thinking?	77
9	Conclusion	81

Preface

The concept of 'having a mind' is one of the key concepts that we use to carve a division of extreme significance into the universe. We say that parts of the universe 'have a mind' and that parts of the universe do not 'have a mind'. This is seemingly a very important distinction as 'having a mind' is surely a valuable thing. One might want to treat parts of the universe that 'have a mind' differently to those parts that do not 'have a mind'. But, what exactly is a mind?

The aim of this book is not to consider whether a computer has a mind, whether a tree has a mind, or whether an atom has a mind; our aim is simply to reflect upon the question of what it means for a mind to exist. To put this slightly differently, our objective is *not* to consider whether there actually is a distinction in the universe between the minded and the non-minded, it is simply to consider what it could possibly mean to assert that such a distinction exists.

Introduction

It is far from clear what it means to 'have a mind'; that is to say, it is far from clear what it means to say that part of the universe is 'mental' whilst part of the universe is 'non-mental.'

According to Herbert Feigl the term 'mental' is precariously vague which means that progress in the mind—body problem requires a study of all of the attributes that are often taken to be 'mental'. He claims that:

> The terms "mental" and "physical" are precariously ambiguous and vague. Hence a

What is a mind?

> first prerequisite for the clarification and the adequate settlement of the main issues [in the mind-body problem] is an analytical study of the meanings of each of the two key terms [1]

> the term "mental" in ordinary and even scientific usage represents a whole family of concepts...special distinctions like "mental$_1$", "mental$_2$", "mental$_3$", etc. are needed in order to prevent confusions [2]

---

[1] Herbert Feigl, *The "Mental" and the "Physical"*, OUP, London, 1967, p. 20.

[2] Herbert Feigl, *The "Mental" and the "Physical"*, OUP, London, 1967, pp. 45-6.

Introduction

In accordance with this view the purpose of this book is to approach the question of what a mind is through considering a number of attributes which are often thought to be mental attributes. The idea that a mind is a central core of human attributes is considered and rejected. Most of the book is spent exploring the opposing idea that having a mind entails having a single attribute; many of these supposedly 'mental' attributes are considered.

Our approach is as follows. Let us suppose that this particular 'mental' attribute exists; is one then inclined to assert that its existence means that a mind exists? If not, then the attribute is seemingly not sufficient for the existence of a mind; there is, or

What is a mind?

could conceivably be, a part of the universe in which this attribute exists but in which a mind does not exist.

The converse supposition will also be used: let us suppose that this particular attribute does not exist, is one inclined to assert that its absence means that a mind does not exist? If not, then the attribute is seemingly not necessary for the existence of a mind.

So, our objective is to identify which attributes we intuitively hold to be necessary and/or sufficient for the existence of a mind. In this way our aim is to cut through the "precarious ambiguity and vagueness" of mental talk and get to the heart of what it really means for a mind to exist.

Mind 1

A central core of human attributes?

When one reflects on what a mind is one of the first conclusions one will reach is surely that it is an attribute that at least most humans possess. This starting 'conclusion' is unproblematic; whatever having a mind entails it is indubitably the case that at least most humans possess this attribute.

However, some people *start out* with a list of attributes that they take to be central to *being a*

What is a mind?

human, and then argue that having these attributes is 'having a mind'. This *is* deeply problematic. For example, Eric Matthews, D. M. Armstrong, and Richard L. Gregory state that:

> To say what we mean by the mental is... a matter of distinguishing a central core of human attributes, activities, processes and so on[3]

> Men have minds, that is to say, they perceive, they have sensations, emotions, beliefs, thoughts, purposes and desires. What is it to have a mind? What is it to perceive, to feel

---

[3] Eric Matthews, *Mind*, Continuum, London, 2005, p. 51.

A central core of human attributes?

emotion, to hold a belief or to have a purpose?[4]

mind a vague term, covering control of intentional behaviour and awareness...learning, memory, perception, emotion, intention, aesthetics, and much more[5]

This conception of what having a mind is is so problematic because it is an *a posteriori* attempt to make sense of one's pre-existing beliefs about what having a mind is. In other words, the advocate of this view will typically believe that humans have

---

[4] D. M. Armstrong, *The Nature of Mind and Other Essays*, St Lucia, University of Queensland Press, 1980, p. 1.

[5] Richard L. Gregory, Ed., *The Oxford Companion to the Mind*, 2nd Edition., Oxford, Oxford University Press, 2004, p. xviii.

minds and things such as stones and tables don't have minds; in order to justify this belief they devise a list of attributes which they believe humans possess but that stones and tables lack. Once this 'central core' of human attributes has been created it is then asserted that these attributes – attributes which stones and tables are believed to lack, but which humans don't lack – are 'mental' attributes.

When this 'central core' of human attributes has been created, and asserted to be what 'having a mind' is, the possession of 'a mind' can then be analogically extended to some non-human parts of the universe. So, when one perceives a particular part of the universe – a part which one may call a

A central core of human attributes?

'cat' – the movement patterns which one perceives may cause one to conclude that a 'cat' also possesses the attributes within the 'central core' to some extent and that it therefore also possesses a mind.

This approach to what a mind is clearly begs the question against those who claim that minds pervade the universe. In other words, if one just stipulates that having a mind is having a 'central core of *human* attributes' then, by definition, the universe will be divided into the 'minded' and the 'non-minded'. The vast majority of the universe will be assumed to be non-minded simply because it is not sufficiently 'human-like'.

What is a mind?

There is an additional and much more fundamental problem with the 'central core' view. The view, as we have seen, is grounded in a *definitional division of the universe;* but how exactly should the division be made? Those who reject the 'central core' view will rightly ask for justification as to why exactly this list of attributes constitute a mind rather than a slightly different list – why not a longer list, or a shorter list? In other words, the objection is that the list is wholly arbitrary. Fred might have a list of five attributes, Sally might have a list of four attributes, and Tom might have a list of ten attributes. Furthermore, every few days Tom might change his mind; one day his 'central core' of mental attributes has ten members, a few days later it has increased to

A central core of human attributes?

eleven, and a week later it has decreased to seven attributes! This is clearly a hopeless approach to the question of what it means to 'have a mind'.

Furthermore, the worry will be, as we have already seen, that the list is devised *a posteriori* in an attempt to make sense of one's pre-reflective beliefs about which entities have minds. This is deeply problematic because one's pre-reflective beliefs are derived from one's inevitably constrained perceptions of one's surroundings (see my book "Conceptions of the Universe" for more on this).

If one is to sensibly approach the question of what a mind is then one needs a conceptualisation of mind that *precedes* its attribution to *specific parts* of

What is a mind?

the universe. The opposite approach of asserting that *humans have a collection of attributes* and that the possession of this collection is 'having a mind' is a futile exercise.

Mind 2

Freedom?

> The second volume of *The Life of the Mind* will be devoted to the faculty of the Will and, by implication, to the problem of Freedom[6]

Could there be a single attribute which if it exists means that 'a mind' exists? In this chapter, and the following chapters, such a possibility will be explored. Our concern in this chapter is the possibil-

---

[6] Hannah Arendt, *The Life of the Mind – Two/Willing*, Secker and Warburg, London, 1978, p. 3.

ity that if freedom exists then 'a mind' exists. The attribute of freedom is often envisioned to be a hallmark of a mind; the 'minded' possesses the attribute of freedom, whilst the 'non-minded' lacks this attribute. What exactly is freedom? Sometimes the concept of freedom is envisioned as freedom from constraint; on this view a human who is put in a straightjacket and kept in solitary confinement is devoid of freedom. This is not the conception of freedom which one is referring to when one asserts that freedom is the hallmark of a mind. One would not say that a particular human had a mind at t_1, and a moment later at t_2 was devoid of a mind solely because they had been put into a straightjacket. Rather, to say that freedom is the hallmark of a mind is to envision that a part of the world has *alternative possible future states even if that part encountered identical future surroundings*. In other words, a part of the world lacks freedom if its states are *wholly determined* by its surrounding world, whilst a part of the world has freedom if its states are self-determining *despite* its surrounding world.

Now, it is a trivial truth that one has no way of knowing whether all of the states in the world are wholly determined by their surroundings. The entire universe could be pervaded by freedom; contrarily, the entire universe could be wholly devoid of freedom. So, it is possible that the entire universe could be wholly devoid of freedom, a scenario which

What is a mind?

obviously entails that one and one's family and lifelong friends are, and always have been, wholly devoid of freedom. If one accepted that this was so would one then feel inclined to assert that one, one's family, and one's lifelong friends lacked a mind? This conclusion would be a most bizarre one to reach; one would surely conclude that irrespective of whether or not these humans possessed freedom that they still possessed a mind.

To be clear, in this scenario one's family and friends having feelings, emotions, thoughts, and normal human behaviour, it is just that all of their thoughts and movements are determined. The absence of freedom in this scenario surely does not entail the absence of a mind. A mind is an attribute that one wants to assert that these humans possess irrespective of whether or not they possess the attribute of freedom. Therefore, the only sensible conclusion to reach is that freedom is not necessary for the existence of a mind because minds could clearly exist even if determinism is true.

Mind 3

Feeling States?

Many people who philosophise about the mind, interestingly, in giving an example of something 'mental', tend to concentrate on pain sensations... But they do not seem to be central to what we think of as 'mental'.[7]

Animals, whether or not they can reason, certainly have minds in the sense of having feelings of pain and pleasure[8]

---

[7] Eric Matthews, *Mind*, Continuum, London, 2005, p. 50.

[8] Eric Matthews, *Mind*, Continuum, London, 2005, p. 76.

Feeling states?

states of mind – headaches[9]

As Eric Matthews notes, many people who philosophise about 'having a mind' argue that feeling states of pain and pleasure are paradigmatic mental attributes. Matthews claims that such states are not *central* to 'having a mind'. The question before us here is: Does the existence of such states have *anything* to do with having a mind? The proposed answer is that the existence of a feeling state, a state which *can be judged as either 'painful'*

---

[9] John Heil, *Philosophy of Mind: A Contemporary Introduction*, Routledge, 1998, p. 61.

What is a mind?

or 'pleasurable' has nothing whatsoever to do with having a mind.

Let us consider the possibility that when two hydrogen atoms and an oxygen atom interact to form a water molecule a certain feeling state is generated; let us refer to this particular feeling state as an 'htwoain' state. If this strikes one as implausible one should keep in mind that there is no compulsion *either* that the existence of a feeling state be accompanied by awareness of that state, *or* that a feeling state be accompanied by a judgement as to whether the state is 'good' (pleasurable) or 'bad' (painful).

Feeling states?

Now, the issue before us is as follows: if a solitary 'htwoain' feeling state existed would one feel inclined to assert that a mind exists? As already stated there need be no awareness of the existence of the state or any thought concerning the state – that it is either painful or pleasurable; there is just a tiny part of the universe which has a particular feeling state. The answer is, surely, that one would not feel inclined to assert that a mind exists. To say that a mind exists is not to say that a solitary 'htwoain' state exists; whatever a mind is it must be more than this.

A less abstract example than the 'htwoain' scenario is the possibility of the existence of bodily pains which exist outside of the awareness of the human whose body those pains are located in. According to David Rosenthal:

> If we are intermittently unaware of a pain by being distracted from it, we feel the pain only intermittently; similarly with its hurting and our being in pain. Still, it is natural to speak of having had a pain that lasted throughout the day, and even to say that one was not always aware of that pain. This provides evidence that commonsense countenances the existence of nonconscious pains. Feeling pains and having them seem equivalent only

Feeling states?

because of our lack of interest in the nonconscious cases.[10]

In this 'pain without awareness' scenario feeling states – states which would be judged to be 'painful' *if* one was aware of them – exist in the absence of awareness of their existence. A similar question arises as with the 'htwoain' scenario: Would one want to assert that the existence of a solitary feeling state in a human body which exists without any awareness of its existence, but which one would judge as 'painful' if one was aware of it, entails the

---

[10] David Rosenthal, "A Theory of Consciousness", in *The Nature of Consciousness*, Ed. N. Block, O. Flanagan, G. Guzeldere, MIT Press, London, 1997, p. 732.

What is a mind?

existence of a mind? Again, I take it that the answer is obviously no. To say that such a state exists and to say that a mind exists is to say two entirely different things.

Our conclusion is that feeling states are *not sufficient* for the existence of a mind. Are feeling states *necessary* for the existence of a mind? Let us imagine that a human is wholly devoid of feeling states, but that other than this lack the human is a typical human; this 'feelingless' human would still be acting and thinking/reasoning in the same manner as all typical humans. Is the 'feelingless' human devoid of a mind? The denial of a mind to this human would be hard to defend; it is seemingly obvious that they have a mind because they are able to think/reason and act like a 'feeling' human. This means that feeling states are not necessary for the existence of a mind.

Of course, one could object that thinking itself entails feeling states/'what-it-is-likeness'; if this were so, then clearly there would be a contradiction – the 'feelingless' human thinks but is also devoid of feelings, so if thinking entails feeling the 'feelingless' human would be impossible.

I take it to be obvious that thinking and feeling are two entirely different things and that, therefore, the 'feelingless' human is a theoretical possibility. So, if one believes that thinking is sufficient for

What is a mind?

'having a mind' this doesn't mean that 'having a mind' entails the existence of feeling. Given this, the conclusion stands that feeling states are neither necessary nor sufficient for the existence of a mind.

Mind 4

Perception?

Men have minds, that is to say, they perceive[11]

mind a vague term, covering...perception[12]

As the above claims from Armstrong and Gregory make clear, some people believe that perceiving is a 'mental' attribute. This is surely a highly dubious

---

[11] D. M. Armstrong, *The Nature of Mind*, Cornell University Press, 1981, p. 1.

[12] Richard L. Gregory, Ed., *The Oxford Companion to the Mind*, 2nd Edition, Oxford, Oxford University Press, 2004, p. xviii.

What is a mind?

belief. It is very plausible to claim that the parts of the universe that have a mind *also* have states of perception. However, to say that a part of the universe has a mind *because* it contains states of perception – that perception is a 'mental' attribute – is a very different claim.

Does one really want to say that if a state of perception exists that this entails that a mind exists? To illuminate the point – it is intelligible that an atom might perceive its surroundings but be wholly devoid of thought/feeling/freedom/awareness etc.; if one asserts that perception is a 'mental attribute' then one is asserting that this atom has a mind. I don't really think that one would want to assert that every atom has 'a mind' simply because atoms perceive their surroundings.

There are different views one can have of perception. If one starts from the assumption that only minds can perceive then one will clearly assert that the existence of a state of perception entails that a mind exists. This assumption seems to arise from a 'thick' view of perception according to which a state of perception is necessarily accompanied by other attributes; so, one might believe that a state of perception must be accompanied by awareness, or one might believe that perception is necessarily concept entailing. If one believes that to have a mind *is* to possess awareness, and that perception entails awareness, then one will clearly believe that to have a state of perception is to have a mind.

Similarly, if one believes that to have a mind is to possess concepts, and that perception is necessarily concept-entailing, then one will believe that to have a state of perception is to have a mind.

Conversely, if one believes in a 'thin' view of perception according to which there can be perception without awareness *and* perception is wholly devoid of concepts then one will probably not feel particularly inclined to assert that the existence of a state of perception entails that a mind exists.

So, if the 'thin' view of perception is correct then the existence of a state of perception is seemingly not sufficient for the existence of a mind; I take it that the 'thin' view of perception is correct. The first reason for believing the 'thin' view to be correct is that it is increasingly widely acknowledged that perception can exist without awareness. The second reason for believing the 'thin' view to be correct is that perception is not concept-entailing. Of course, one could have a conception of a concept that is so 'thin' that perception *is* concept-entailing, but if this were so the 'thinness' of concepts would result in a 'thin' view of perception; that is to say, the conception of a concept would be so watered down as to not make one feel inclined to assert that the existence of such a concept entailed that a mind existed.

What is a mind?

Let us briefly consider why perception does not entail concepts in anything other than the 'thinnest' of senses, at the most. When we consider in general terms what a perception is then it is clear that a perception is simply an acquisition of information about the surroundings; that is, to perceive is to be affected by the surroundings in some way. This is what perception is. Those who advocate the 'thick' view of perception are entangling perception up with other states such as the awareness of the perception, or a thought concerning the perception.

On the 'thin' view of perception it is perfectly intelligible that all parts of the universe perceive. To see how this can be so let us consider the part of the universe that humans call 'a thermometer'. On the 'thin' view of perception a thermometer contains states of perception; this is because a functioning thermometer acquires information about its surroundings. The thermometer's perceptions are 'thin' because they are, let us suppose, unaccompanied by awareness or concepts. What exactly does it mean to assert that a thermometer contains states of perception? Primarily it just means that a thermometer is acquiring information from its surroundings.

Furthermore, a thermometer is clearly acquiring a specific kind of information, a kind which it responds to; it could have been designed to acquire a different kind of information from its surroundings

What is a mind?

such as atmospheric pressure; if this were so one would call it a mercurial barometer rather than a mercurial thermometer. This means that the thermometer is dividing up its surroundings in some way when it perceives those surroundings. If one was to adopt a 'thin' conception of concepts then one could argue that this dividing up of the surroundings equated to a concept. This dividing up would be analogous to when a dolphin divides up its surroundings through echo location, and to when a human visually perceives a paper clip. Let us assume that this process of dividing up does not entail awareness, and that it does not entail thought; if it is a process that is worthy of the name 'concept' then concepts are clearly very 'thin' indeed.

Perception?

On the 'thin' view of perception concepts *as we ordinarily think of them* are the products not of perception but of thought. It is in thought that divisions within one's surroundings (i.e. perceptions) are contrasted and grouped together into families of similarity. One can perceive the division in the world that is a paper clip without having the concept 'paper clip'. It is a process of thought that generates the concept 'paper clip' rather than the perceptual dividing up of the surroundings. This sharp disparity between perception and concepts is argued for by E. J. Lowe who states that:

> pigeons can be trained to discriminate visually between triangles and squares, but it

would be extravagant to suggest that they therefore possess the concepts of triangularity and squareness. For example, we should not attribute possession of the concept of a *tree* to someone unless we are prepared to attribute to that person certain general beliefs concerning trees, such as that trees are living things which grow from the ground and have branches, roots and leaves. The mere ability to discriminate visually between trees and other objects, such as rocks, and to engage in distinctive behaviour with respect to them, such as nest-building, is not enough to constitute possession of the concept of a tree.[13]

---

[13] E. J. Lowe, *An introduction to the philosophy of mind*, Cam-

This view clearly chimes with the 'thin' view of perception which has been advocated in this chapter. The pigeons undoubtedly perceive the world because they are discriminating between triangles and squares; however, this perceptual discriminatory ability does not *in itself* require the possession of the concepts of triangularity and squareness. If the 'thin' view of perception defended here is correct then it seems that the existence of a state of perception is not sufficient for the existence of a mind.

One would not want to say that a thermometer possessed a mind *because* it contained states of perception. Similarly, one would not want to say that

---

bridge University Press, 2000, p. 182.

What is a mind?

a human possessed a mind *because* it contained states of perception.

Is the existence of a state of perception *necessary* for the existence of a mind? Let us imagine that a human is wholly devoid of states of perception, but that they are still capable of a high level of thinking/reasoning; a level analogous to a typical human. Would one want to assert that this 'perceptionless' human lacked a mind? The denial of a mind to this human would surely be unacceptable; it is seemingly obvious that they do have a mind. Given this, states of perception are neither necessary nor sufficient for the existence of a mind.

Mind 5

Intentionality?

Philosophers have long been concerned with the phenomenon of intentionality, which has seemed to many to be a fundamental feature of mental states[14]

The phenomenon of intentionality – of aboutness – is often envisioned as a fundamental mark of a mind. Franz Brentano claimed that it is intentionality that divides the 'mental' from the 'non-mental' as

---

[14] Richard L. Gregory, Ed. *The Oxford Companion to the Mind*, Oxford, Oxford University Press, 1987, p. 383.

all and only mental phenomena exhibit intentionality. This focus on intentionality is surely unhelpful because the notion is very vague. To say that if a state exists that is 'about' or 'directed towards' another state then a mind exists is not only vague it is implausible.

The vagueness of the bounds of intentionality start with phenomena such as tree rings – are tree rings intentional states which are 'about' the age of the tree? Perhaps they are not because they are instances of *derived intentionality* rather than *original intentionality*; derived intentionality being a state of intentionality that requires a perceiver in order to exist.

Intentionality?

What about states of perception such as the visual perception of a paper clip? This certainly seems to be a state of *original intentionality* – there is a perceptual state which is *directed towards* a paper clip. But, as we saw in the previous chapter, to say that such a perceptual state exists is *not* to say that a mind exists. So, this instance of *original intentionality* does not entail that a mind exists.

It is plausible that all thinking is intentional, and that thinking is necessary and sufficient for the existence of a mind, but in this case it is thinking which is the mark of a mind; intentionality being a 'red herring' – not the mark of anything. The

What is a mind?

phenomenon of thinking will be considered in *Chapter 8*.

These sentiments – that intentionality is a 'red herring' chimes with the views of philosophers who advocate the 'physical intentionality' thesis. According to this view all chemical and physical interactions have intentionality because they are directed towards particular outcomes. For example, George Molnar states:

> I think that the Brentano thesis is basically mistaken...I accept the intentionality of the mental, and go on to argue that something *very much like* intentionality is a pervasive

and ineliminable feature of the physical world.[15]

This belief – that intentionality is more pervasive in the world than the minded – has inevitably caused many philosophers, including Molnar, to conclude that intentionality cannot be sufficient for the existence of a mind. Of course, another option is to embrace physical intentionality and to argue that this means that minds pervade all of the physical. So, if the physical intentionality thesis is true this means either that intentionality is not a mark of a mind or that minds pervade all of the physical.

---

[15] George Molnar, *Powers: A Study in Metaphysics*, Oxford, Oxford University Press, 2003, p. 61.

What is a mind?

If one accepts the physical intentionality thesis then it is unlikely (as Molnar concludes) that one will believe that the existence of a state of intentionality is sufficient for the existence of a mind. This means that the possibility of physical intentionality should multiply our pre-existing doubts that intentionality is sufficient for the existence of a mind.

However, even if one asserted that the physical intentionality thesis is false one would still not feel compelled to assert that if a state of intentionality exists that this means that a mind exists. When one reflects on the question of why one believes that at least most humans possess a mind one is most unlikely to conclude that it is *because they contain states that are directed towards other states*. One might plausibly assert that most humans possess a mind because they have awareness or because they think. However, if one concluded that most humans possess a mind *because* they *contain states that are directed towards other states* then one is opening the door to the possibility that large parts (or all) of the universe contains minds.

The most sensible conclusion to reach is surely the one reached by Molnar — that *even if* physical intentionality is true this doesn't mean that all of the physical is pervaded by 'minds'. Our conclusion is thus that intentionality is not sufficient for the

What is a mind?

existence of a mind – to say that a mind exists is to say more than that states of directedness exist.

Is intentionality *necessary* for the existence of a mind? This is an open question. As we have already noted, it is plausible that thinking entails intentionality and that thinking is necessary and sufficient for the existence of a mind. If this were so, then the existence of mind/thought would entail the existence of intentionality, but intentionality would clearly not be the mark of a mind – there could be intentionality without a mind. However, it is also possible that the existence of thinking does not necessarily entail the existence of states of intentionality; if this were so then intentionality would not be necessary for the existence of a mind.

Whichever way you look at it intentionality is not the mark of a mind; it is a 'red herring'.

Mind 6

Awareness?

mind a vague term, covering...awareness[16]

It is often claimed that there is a link between awareness and mind. In the above passage Gregory claims that mind is a term 'covering' awareness. The aim of this chapter is to suggest that there is, in fact, no such link.

---

[16] Richard L. Gregory, Ed., *The Oxford Companion to the Mind*, 2nd Edition, Oxford, Oxford University Press, 2004, p. xviii.

Awareness?

When a human is wholly devoid of awareness, that is to say, when a human is in an 'unconscious' state, one might reasonably assert that they still possess a mind. Conversely, it is possible that states of awareness might exist in the absence of a mind. The existence of a mind without awareness, and of awareness without a mind, would entail that awareness is neither necessary nor sufficient for the existence of a mind.

Let us consider whether a human who is wholly devoid of awareness has a mind. First of all, let us consider the 'sleep' scenario. When a human is sleeping and wholly devoid of awareness then this human presumably still contains a mind. Why is

What is a mind?

this? One possibility is that they contain a mind because they contain a thinking brain. Another possibility is that they contain a mind because they contain the capacity for awareness. If this human has a mind solely because they contain a thinking brain then neither awareness nor the capacity for awareness is necessary for a mind to exist. However, if they possess a mind because they contain the capacity for awareness then although there can be a mind without awareness it would be the capacity for awareness which would be the hallmark of a mind.

Let us now consider the 'coma' scenario. In this scenario there is a human which never contains awareness because they have permanently lost the

Awareness?

capacity for awareness; yet this human still contains a thinking brain. This 'coma' scenario is differentiated from the 'sleep' scenario because in the latter scenario the human still contains the capacity for awareness, whereas in the 'coma' scenario this capacity has been lost. The question is whether the human in the 'coma' scenario still possesses a mind. In other words: Is thinking sufficient for the existence of a mind? The most reasonable answer to this question, I suggest, is that thinking is sufficient for the existence of a mind irrespective of whether or not it is accompanied by awareness, and irrespective of whether or not the capacity exists for there to be awareness of this thinking. If this is right, then the

What is a mind?

reason that the 'sleeping' human has a mind is that they possess a thinking brain.

As a contrast to these examples of mind without awareness it is worth considering the possibility that a human could have both a mind and awareness continuously. This possibility has supposedly been realised in various humans such as Thai Ngoc who claims to have been in a continuous state of awareness for thirty-three years[17].

These various scenarios imply that there are several possible relationships between mind and awareness, and suggest that whilst the two phenom-

---

[17] http://thanhniennews.com/features/?catid=10&newsid=12673 [accessed 10 February 2010].

Awareness?

ena may co-occur, that they are fundamentally different phenomena.

How might one object to the conclusion that mind and awareness are fundamentally different phenomena? One could insist that without the capacity for awareness there cannot be a mind. This means that in the 'coma' scenario one has three options. One could reject the assumption that thinking is sufficient for a mind to exist; one could reject the assumption that there can be thinking without awareness; or one could reject the assumption that the capacity for awareness has been permanently lost. Given the plausibility of the first

What is a mind?

two assumptions, the most plausible option is to assert that the capacity for awareness remains.

However, whilst this option is the most plausible one it is also deeply problematic. Let us consider a situation in which one is observing another human who moves from a state of seemingly having awareness to a state of 'sleep', and who then several hours later moves back to a state of seeming awareness again. It would be quite right to assert that when they were not aware they contained the capacity for awareness. However, in the 'coma' scenario the physical arrangement of the world which provides the capacity for awareness in typical humans does not exist. It is the absence of this capacity which is the *cause* of the 'coma' situation. So, to say that the capacity for awareness still exists in the 'coma' scenario is *really* to say that a physical arrangement of the world exists which if it was arranged slightly differently would have the capacity for awareness. In other words, the human in the 'coma' scenario has undergone a change in the physical arrangement of their brain which means that they are continuously devoid of awareness but *if* this physical change was reversed *then* they would be able to contain awareness. The problem with this is that it is very difficult to defend the idea of a 'slightly' different arrangement. If it is acceptable to assert that an arrangement which would have the capacity for awareness if it was 'slightly' different is an arrangement which has the capacity for awareness then why shouldn't one be able to assert that an arrangement which is 'slightly more' different also has this capacity. This leads straight to a reduction (absurdity) in which such arrangements as a mound of sand have the capacity for awareness. Either a capacity exists or it doesn't and in the 'coma' scenario it doesn't.

Let us turn to the possibility that states of awareness could exist in the absence of a mind. There seems to be no reason to rule out this possibility. After all, it is intelligible to suppose that a state could exist which is a state of 'simple awareness'. This state, whilst being a state of awareness, is a very simple state such as the awareness of a simple feeling state, or the awareness of a particular colour. These are simple states because they are unchanging and they do not entail thought. These states could conceivably exist in various parts of the universe; for example, they could exist when certain chemical interactions occur in the atmosphere. If these chemical interactions are instances of 'simple awareness' then one would surely not claim that this meant that the chemical interactions were minds. Even if states of 'simple awareness' do not actually exist it is useful to consider them because one would surely not want to assert that if a state of 'simple awareness' existed that this meant that a mind

What is a mind?

existed. To say that a mind exists is to say more than that a state of 'simple awareness' exists.

What is our conclusion? It is possible that a mind can exist in the absence of awareness so awareness is not necessary for the existence of a mind. It is also possible that a mind can exist in the absence of the capacity for awareness so the capacity for awareness is not necessary for the existence of a mind. Furthermore, it is also possible that awareness could exist in the absence of a mind so awareness is not sufficient for the existence of a mind.

Mind 7

The Inner Cause of Certain Movements in Suitable Circumstances?

perhaps what we mean by a mental state is some state of the person that, under suitable circumstances, *brings about* a certain range of behaviour. Perhaps mind can be defined not as behaviour, but rather as the inner *cause* of behaviour... I believe that this is the

What is a mind?

true account, or, at any rate, a true first account, of what we mean by a mental state.[18]

According to Armstrong having a 'mind' is having *inner states which under suitable circumstances cause certain types of movements*. This will probably strike one as a slightly odd definition of a 'mind'. This 'oddness' arises because the *starting assumption* underlying the definition is that 'a mind causes movement'. This *starting assumption* is very uninformative as certain movements of a human presumably do not result from a mind; it is also very unpersuasive because one surely presumes that a

---

[18] D. M. Armstrong, *The Nature of Mind*, Cornell University Press, 1981, p. 7.

human who is totally paralysed can still have a mind. In order to deal with these points and create a not obviously false conceptualisation of mind the *starting assumption* gets qualifications added to it. So, a mind only causes "certain" movements and it only causes these movements in "suitable circumstances". In this way a mind becomes *the inner cause of certain movements in suitable circumstances.*

If one has a much more plausible starting assumption – that to have a mind is to think, then one can have a much more appealing conceptualisation of what a mind is – *where there is thinking there is a mind.* There is no need to add qualifications to this definition because it is simply the case that if there is thinking then one wants to say that a mind exists. The fact that Armstrong's 'mind is movement' thesis needs to be qualified to make it *more* plausible actually makes this conception of mind *less* plausible. Of course, Armstrong's inner states are actually thought states. The implausibility of Armstrong's account arises because of the stipulation that to have a mind is for these states (in 'suitable circumstances') to cause movement.

Let us further consider the phenomena of 'mind' and 'movement'. Some humans have a medical condition which is known as total locked-in syndrome. In this state a human is completely paralysed and is therefore unable to move in any way, yet apart from this inability to move they resemble a typical human in all other respects. If humans in this condition have a mind, which they surely do, then movement is not necessary for the existence of a mind.

Conversely, it also seems obviously true that a certain pattern of movements is not *in itself* sufficient for the existence of a mind; one will only want to assert that a particular pattern of movements is sufficient for the existence of a mind if one believes that there is thought 'behind' this pattern. If a mind is the thing which is *behind* a movement pattern then a mind is obviously *not the movement pattern itself.* That there is no connection between having a mind and movement has been argued for by Galen Strawson who states that:

> The Weather Watchers are a race of sentient, intelligent creatures. They are distributed about the surface of the planet, rooted to the ground, profoundly interested in the local weather. They have sensations, thoughts, emotions, beliefs, desires. They possess a conception of an objective, spatial world. But they are constitutionally incapable of any sort of behaviour, as this is ordinarily understood. They lack the necessary physiology. Their mental lives have no other-observable effects.

They are not even disposed to behave in any way.[19]

Strawson is surely right to claim that despite the lack of "other-observable effects" the Weather Watchers possess a mind. So, let us conclude. It is entirely plausible to assert that the mind of a human is the inner cause of certain movements in suitable circumstances. However, this doesn't mean that *what it is to be a mind* is just to be something that is the inner cause of certain movements in suitable circumstances. Rather, *what it is to be a mind* has nothing to do with movement – *where there is thinking there is mind*. So, the existence of a mind

---

[19] Galen Strawson, *Mental Reality,* MIT Press, London, 1994, p. 251.

What is a mind?

and the existence of movement are two utterly unrelated phenomena.

Here we have another 'red herring'.

Mind 8

Thinking?

Reason, Descartes says, is a 'universal instrument'... That is, it does not respond specifically to specific stimuli, but varyingly to varying stimuli.[20]

I suggest that if part of the universe is thinking then this part of the universe possesses a mind. More than this, to say that a mind exists is to say nothing more than to say that thinking exists. The idea that a

---

[20] Eric Matthews, *Mind*, Continuum, London, 2005, p. 73.

What is a mind?

mind could exist in the complete absence of thought is a contradiction in terms. Thinking is both necessary and sufficient for the existence of a mind. Whilst this seems obviously true (I hope you agree) the exact nature of thinking is far from clear. What exactly is thinking? Stephen Priest claims that:

> Thinking may take place in language, in an ordinary language such as English, or in an artificial language such as logical notation. Some thinking also takes place in neither of those media but in mental images[21]

---

[21] Stephen Priest, *Theories of the Mind*, Penguin Books, London, 1991, p. 213.

Thinking?

Thinking is clearly a complex phenomenon. It involves many issues such as the relationship between thought, language and concepts, and the issue of whether thought involves 'what-it-is-likeness'. An initial definition of thinking is that thinking is a process of reasoning. Another way of putting this is to say that thinking is the consideration of possibilities. This initial definition raises a lot of questions. For example: Is a chess computer thinking when it is 'considering' the possible moves it can make?

This is an interesting question, the answer is uncertain. Attempting to answer this question is outside the scope of this book. Recall, the aim of this book is not to make progress on the issue of which

What is a mind?

parts of the universe have a mind, or have a particular attribute. Our aim is simply to establish that if thinking exists then a mind exists. So, *if* a chess computer is thinking *then* it possesses a mind.

9

Conclusion

The purpose of this book has been to answer the following question: What is a mind? The view that a mind is a central core of human attributes was considered and rejected. Several attributes which are often taken to be 'mental' attributes have been considered – freedom, feeling states, perception, intentionality, awareness, and the inner cause of certain movements in suitable circumstances – and it has been suggested that none of these attributes is sufficient for the existence of a mind.

What is a mind?

Furthermore, it has been suggested that none of these attributes – with the possible exception of intentionality – is necessary for the existence of a mind. It has been suggested that thinking is both necessary and sufficient for the existence of a mind; this means that *if all* thought entails intentionality *then* intentionality would be necessary for the existence of a mind. Our conclusion is therefore that if thinking exists a mind exists, and if thinking does not exist then a mind does not exist. Thinking is the sole attribute of a mind. This means that all of the other attributes that we have considered are not, in any meaningful sense, 'mental' attributes.

To 'have a mind' is to think.

Other books by the author:

What is Creativity? : Originality, Art & Invention
(2011)

Conceptions of the Universe : How our conceptions of reality arise from the limitations of our perceptual apparatus (2011)